LOVE
STORY

Also by Glen Scrivener:

3 2 1
The Story of God, the World and You

Four Kinds of Christmas
Which are You?

Divine Comedy – Human Tragedy
What is Life?

Reading Between the Lines (Volume 1)
Old Testament Daily Readings

Reading Between the Lines (Volume 2)
New Testament Daily Readings

Glen Scrivener

LOVE STORY

*The myth
that really happened*

10 Publishing
a division of 10 of those.com

First published in Great Britain in 2017.

British Library Cataloguing in Publication Data
A record for this book is available from the British Library

ISBN: 978-1-911272-37-3

Designed and typeset by Pete Barnsley (CreativeHoot.com)

Printed in Denmark by Nørhaven

10Publishing, a division of 10ofthose.com
Unit C, Tomlinson Road, Leyland, PR25 2DY, England

Email: info@10ofthose.com
Website: www.10ofthose.com

CONTENTS

TRUE STORY

… When all looked lost, their tragedy turned to comedy: the dragon was slain, the wicked king was overthrown, the quest was completed, the heroes returned, the princess was saved and she married the knight. So they all lived happily ever after. The End.

What do you make of fairy tales? C.S. Lewis loved them. He spent much of his life studying and teaching the ancient Greek, Roman and Norse myths, and he went on to write some of the most popular fantasies of all time – the Chronicles of Narnia series (*The Lion, the Witch and the Wardrobe*, and so on). In many ways myths were Lewis's life, yet he had mixed feelings about them. He was enthralled by the stories, but at the same time he considered them as escapism – as *mere* fantasies. One night, though, he had a conversation that changed everything.

On 19 September 1931, Lewis was speaking with his great friend J.R.R. Tolkien, author of *The Lord of the Rings*. Mr Narnia was chatting with Mr Middle Earth! At this point Tolkien was a Christian but Lewis was not. In fact Lewis had a big problem with Christianity, namely the Easter story. He could understand that people might believe in a God. He could appreciate that God might want people to live in a certain way. That kind of religion sounded reasonable enough. But that isn't Christianity. Christians insist on telling a *story* – all about God coming to earth to die for his creatures. More than its creeds or rituals or moral codes, it is the Easter *story* that is central for Christians. And that was Lewis's sticking point. He didn't understand how the death and resurrection of Jesus related to the rest of Christianity. What on earth was the point of Easter?

In answer Tolkien directed Lewis back to all the myths he loved. Didn't Lewis appreciate the ancient stories of the dying and rising gods?

Didn't he see how those myths worked on his heart in a profound way? Yes indeed, Lewis was deeply moved by such stories. Well, declared Tolkien, Christianity is the ultimate story of the dying and rising God.

But, Lewis countered, all those stories are just myths. They aren't *true.* In a memorable phrase Lewis called them 'lies breathed through silver' – they are beautiful but ultimately empty.

How would Tolkien respond? Surely he would have to agree with Lewis. No-one could think that fairy tales were real, could they? Tolkien shocked Lewis with his answer: 'No,' said Tolkien, 'they are not lies.'[1] This was earth-shattering for Lewis. If Tolkien was right, then there is such a thing as a *real* fairy tale. There exists a grand story that lies behind all other stories – namely Easter. Easter is the ultimate and original myth – the myth that really happened.

This got Lewis thinking of all the stories he had loved – not only tales of death and resurrection but stories of rags to riches; of defeating the monster; of epic quests; of grand romances; of desperate tragedies; of joyful comedies; of victory snatched from defeat; of the prince marrying the pauper and the happily ever after. These stories resonate with us across the cultures and down the ages. But why? Is there a reason our hearts are tuned to such realities? Might there be a grand, original story that is reflected and refracted in our little stories? And could this explain the centrality of Easter?

THE TRUE MYTH

Within a month of this famous conversation Lewis had all but converted to Christianity. He had begun to see the story of Christ as 'a true myth: a myth working on us in the same way as the others, but with this tremendous difference that it really happened.'[2] In the Gospels – the biblical biographies of Jesus – Lewis said the old myth of the dying God 'comes down from the heaven of legend ... to the earth of history. It *happens* – at a particular day, in a particular place.'[3] All the other myths take place in dreamtime – fairy tales happen, as *Star Wars* begins, 'a long time ago in a galaxy far, far away'. The gods live and die beyond our time and space. However, the Gospels show Jesus living and dying in our world, under the reign of named rulers like Pontius Pilate.[4]

This historical character sets the Jesus story apart from all others. Lewis later wrote, 'As a literary historian, I am perfectly convinced that whatever the Gospels are they are not legends. I have read a great deal of legend and I am quite clear that they are not the same sort of thing.'[5] Legends are set *once upon a time*. You simply cannot answer the question 'when?' about any detail of a legend. You cannot find out *when* the Norse god Thor married his wife or *when* the Hindu deity Krishna fought Kaliya. Those stories are not set in our world of time and space. By way of immense contrast, the Gospels are detailed accounts of people, places and times. Even as they tell the most wonderful story, they are written as serious history.

So we find in the Bible an unparalleled combination: mirroring the claim that God entered the world as man, we see in the Gospels that a great myth has entered history as fact. There is an anchoring of the great stories in our time and space. Just as the gods sacrifice and come to life, so Jesus gave his life and rose again.

Just as the knight comes to slay the dragon, so Jesus came to defeat the powers of evil. Just as the prince comes to marry the pauper, so Jesus came to win his beloved people. Just as the hero comes to complete the quest, so Jesus came on a mission from God. And as he fulfils all these classically heroic roles, Jesus turns rags to riches and tragedy to comedy. Here is the love story that has really happened!

Lewis had thought of myths as silvery lies. When examining the Jesus story, he found it to be solid gold truth. More than this, he found it to be the fulfilment of all other stories. In Jesus – and in particular in the Easter story – Lewis discovered an answer to his heart's cry for meaning, joy, hope and love.

In this book we will explore the Easter story for ourselves. We will examine the weekend of Christ's death and resurrection – events that are traditionally known as the *passion* of Jesus Christ. Christians see Easter as the culmination of God's great love story. As Jesus stoops, suffers, sacrifices and stands again, he is bringing to fulfilment an ages-long romance. *Love Story* is about listening to that romance again.

BACK STORY

SETTING THE SCENE

In the world of comic books, 'origins stories' are vital. They set the scene for what follows, explaining where the heroes and villains have come from. As explanations go, genetic mutations, intergalactic warfare and murdered parents are particular favourites.

Easter has its own origins story to set up the drama. In order to understand Jesus and what he came to do, the Bible has thirty-nine books of back story – what we call 'the Old Testament'. Over centuries the authors wrote about our good beginning, our catastrophic fall and then God's plan to set things straight. This plan

centres on a promised Hero, a Warrior, a Lover.
Let me outline the plot in brief.

IN THE BEGINNING ... LOVE

The first verse of the Bible sets the scene for the
coming adventure, and sets it up as a romance:
'In the beginning God created the heavens and
the earth' (Genesis 1:1).

You won't see this at first glance, but the
two main terms in this verse – 'God' and 'the
heavens and the earth' – are all about love. If you
can handle me getting nerdy about grammar,
I'll show you two hidden nuggets. Trust me,
they're golden!

1. 'GOD'

When it says 'God' here in our English Bibles, it's
actually translating a plural noun. In Hebrew, the
original language of the Old Testament, 'God'
is plural, even though it's always attached to a
singular verb. So the grammar is communicating
that God is a plurality but acts as one. There's
something about God that is multiple and
something about God that's unified. Later,

Christians would call this 'the Trinity'. It's a way of saying that God's life is both plural and united. There's something about God that involves three-ness and something about God that involves one-ness. To think of God we need to think of a loving union of three. These three are the Father, the Son and the Holy Spirit – that's who God is according to the Bible.

If that's hard to understand, think of a community. A community is a communal unity. There are ways that a community is plural and there are ways that it is unified. God is a unified community. The members of the community – the Father, the Son and the Holy Spirit – are united together in unbreakable bonds of love. They simply cannot be without each other. Love is not just something that they do, it is who they are and who they have always been.

Here is the origin of all things – love. Before and beyond our world there is a flow, an almighty dance of Father, Son and Holy Spirit. The ultimate back story is a God who *is* love. No wonder the rest of the story unfolds as a great romance.

2. '... THE HEAVENS AND THE EARTH'

In Hebrew, as in all the Romance languages (those evolving from Latin), nouns have gender. For example, if you did any French at school, you might remember that 'sun' (*le soleil*) is masculine while 'moon' (*la lune*) is feminine. Likewise in the Bible 'heaven' is masculine and 'earth' is feminine. We're meant to think, 'Heaven and earth are made for each other. Those two should get together!' Within the first verse of the Bible we see God's romance going cosmic. The love that begins in God, flows out to heaven and earth.

The love story continues when, on the Bible's second page, we are introduced to man and woman. They face each other like heaven and earth, and they are told to unite. In their union they will 'Be fruitful, and multiply'.[6] Through their love the earth will be filled.

In Genesis chapter 2 we learn their names: Adam and Eve. They are made for each other, literally. And when they are brought together, Adam bursts out in the world's first love poem: 'This is now bone of my bones and flesh of my flesh'.[7] It's a picture of the unity we long for – unity with God, with each other and with the world. Right from the beginning we get a foretaste of the happily ever after.

As the Bible progresses, it sticks to the romance theme. God says he loves his people with a faithful, marital love. But here is the problem: his people are always going astray. As they turn from the God of love, they are not simply described as 'disobedient' or 'sinful'. More profoundly, they are called 'adulterous' and 'unfaithful'. This is loaded language. We are liable to ask, 'What – are we meant to be *married* to God?' Apparently so!

Like earth and heaven, like Eve and Adam, we are called to be united to God in a committed, love relationship. But, as Shakespeare wrote, 'The course of true love never did run smooth.'[8] While God may love us, the question remains whether we will receive or reject that love. The history of the Old Testament proves a universal rule: in general we reject the love we should receive (God's) and pursue other loves that we shouldn't – loves that harm ourselves and others. This is the origin of all our problems.

LOVE SPURNED

Let me tell you about one Old Testament story that sums up the whole. It's about the prophet Hosea. He lived about 750 BC. Essentially the Lord says to Hosea, 'I've got a treat for you. You're going to experience what it feels like to be me in the great love story.' That might sound exciting, but here's what happened. God says to Hosea:

> Go, marry a promiscuous woman and have children with her, for like an adulterous wife this land is guilty of unfaithfulness to the LORD (Hosea 1:2).

The LORD wants Hosea to share in his own experience. What does it feel like for God to be our God? Apparently it feels like being married to a serial adulterer. So this is how Hosea will reflect God's heart: Hosea must marry a prostitute called Gomer.

Hosea does so and, true to form, Gomer does not stick around for long. Soon she leaves the marital home and returns to, of all places, the brothel. Perhaps Hosea thinks he's done his best and now he can return to his bachelor pad and watch endless reruns of *Top Gear*. But the Lord tells him no, he's only just begun. God says to Hosea:

> Go, show your love to your wife again, though she is loved by another man and is an adulteress. Love her as the LORD loves the Israelites, though they turn to other gods (Hosea 3:1).

Hosea actually has to go to the brothel and pay fifteen shekels – the prostitute price – to get his wife back. Can you imagine being Hosea and banging on the brothel door? 'I'm here for Gomer … I'm her husband … I'll pay whatever it costs; I just want her back.'

He is vulnerable; he is exposing himself to great shame; he is putting his heart on the line again with a woman who keeps spurning his love. Why should he pay for his own wife? Why should he endure any of this? Because that's what God is like.

God loves us; he commits himself to us; he is like Hosea. But we are like Gomer. We ignore him; sideline him; and pretend he has no claim over us. In so doing we slink back into the life we've always known. This is what has spoiled the world. We reject God's love and pursue our heart's desires in all the wrong places.

Yet how does God respond? He is the God who pursues us. In fact, as we will see, he will shame himself in order to offer his love again. He will pay for us, redeeming us at great cost, just to have us back in his arms. The whole Old Testament is the promise of a great Hosea – a divine Lover – who will come to claim his people.

THE BIBLE AS ROMANCE

I don't know how you see God. If people believe in God today, they tend to think of him as an impersonal Force. Or he's a Sergeant Major in the sky who barks out orders. Or he's a Heavenly Slave Driver setting us to work. Or he's a Moral Policeman, investigating our performance. Or he's a Cosmic Headmaster saying, 'Must try harder.' But if we've inherited any of those ideas about God, it hasn't been from the Bible.

The Bible tells a love story. There is a romance with one hero at its centre – the Son of God – and he longs to bring us home.

What we see with Easter is the actual coming of this hero in the flesh. In the 'passion' of Jesus Christ we see the ultimate Hosea coming to woo and win back his Gomer.

Jesus comes as a Bridegroom, a Husband, a Royal Prince. His coming is the fulfilment of all the fairy tales. Just as the heroes take epic journeys, so Jesus travels from heaven to earth. Just as they slay the dragon, so Jesus takes on all the forces of evil. Just as they 'get the girl', so Jesus wins our hearts. Just as they turn tragedy to comedy, so Jesus triumphs over death and brings us a 'happily ever after'. Over the next four chapters we will examine four key events in the Easter weekend. From Maundy Thursday to Easter Sunday we will see that these events are part of God's great romance. This 'passion' of Jesus Christ reveals to us that love is at the heart of history, the heart of God, the heart of all reality. The God of the Easter story is not looking for soldiers, slaves or moralists. He's not looking for good intentions, good efforts or good works. He's looking for Gomers to come home.

3

LOVE STOOPS

'What would make you believe in God?' I put this question to a self-professed atheist. He'd clearly been asked it before because he had a ready-made reply: 'If God rearranged the stars in the sky so they spelt out the ten commandments, then I'd believe.'

I don't know where you would set the bar for evidence of God but my friend set it to galactic heights. Yet as he made his request for star realignment, a couple of thoughts sparked in my brain at once. (I'd like to point out that this is unusual. I normally average a couple of thoughts per month, but I was on my fifth coffee that day and – as we'll see – miracles do happen ...)

Thought number one involved a half-remembered quote from an old sage. It goes something like this: if the stars came out just once every thousand years, we would consider it the most astonishing miracle. The fact they come out every night makes us, strangely, more dismissive than awestruck. Is it possible, therefore, that the stars are *already* providing an astonishing witness to God's glory?

In fact, before we ask the stars to reorder themselves, it's worth appreciating the astounding intricacy of their current arrangement. It turns out that the very existence of the stars, and of our being here to 'read' them, is far more improbable than having the Milky Way spell out a message. If you Google 'the fine-tuning of the universe', you will discover that, in order for life to exist, the ordering of the heavens must be so precise that it staggers belief. It's not just that my existence is on a knife edge; it's not just *the earth*'s existence that is perilously balanced; the *whole cosmos* is perched on this knife edge.

The stars are already crying out to us. As King David wrote 3000 years ago, 'The heavens declare the glory of God'.[9] The more we learn about those heavens, the more those words ring true. My atheist friend wanted the heavens to spell out the ten commandments, such as 'Thou shalt not kill'. But what is far more improbable (and far more important) is the fact that the heavens themselves *do not kill*. Amazingly, against all the odds, the arrangement of the heavens permits life. And if a sceptic squinted up at the Milky Way and did see Hebrew letters written there, that would only be a cheap parlour trick piggybacking on the real and gargantuan wonder. The wonder is that there *is* such a galaxy and that there *is* such a squinting sceptic.

So that was my first thought. I was ready to say to my friend, 'You don't need to wonder how you would respond to a jaw-dropping miracle. You're living in one.' But just as I was about to say this, I had a change of heart. Another thought occurred to me, and this was the one I actually voiced. I asked my friend, 'If God did do what you asked – if he rearranged galaxies just to tell you to behave – would you like such a God?'

His reply was instant and impassioned: 'No, I certainly wouldn't like him. But that's not the point. I don't think I could ever like God, but if he proved his existence beyond reasonable doubt, I would have to believe.'

At this point, ironically, my friend and I were close to full agreement. The God he was prepared to consider was a God who *neither of us* liked very much – a superpower, who would flex his cosmic muscles just to make us bow. Such a God, who shows his strength by writing commands in the sky, might force our obedience; he might win a grudging acknowledgement; but he could never win our hearts.

Crucially, though, the God of the Bible is different. He is the God of the ultimate love story. He does not press down on this world to show us who's boss. He shows up in the deepest pit, alongside his suffering people. Rather than write his laws in the stars, he descends to a manger – even to a cross. While we sceptics squint at the stars and demand a sign, this God crops up right under our noses as a bleeding sacrifice. Why? Because love stoops.

THE POSTURE OF GOD

What would it look like to see God? Would the stars be rearranged? Would it involve heavenly fireworks? Jesus says to see God we need only to look at him. This is an extraordinary thing to say, but Jesus is insistent. In John's Gospel we read that right at the outset of the Easter weekend – on the day that's come to be known as Maundy Thursday – Jesus points to himself and says:

The one who looks at me is seeing the one who sent me (John 12:45).

Anyone who has seen me has seen the Father (John 14:9).

It's a way of saying, 'Do you want to see God? Keep looking directly at me.' So all eyes are on Jesus this Thursday night. And what does he do to reveal the very heart of divinity? He stoops:

Jesus knew that the Father had put all things under his power, and that he had come from God and was returning to God; so he got up from the meal, took off his outer clothing, and wrapped a towel round his waist. After that, he poured water into a basin and began to wash his disciples' feet, drying them with the towel that was wrapped round him (John 13:3–5).

Verse three tells us who Jesus is. He's the Son of the Father on a mission from God – to bring us home. That's quite a piece of self-understanding, wouldn't you say? If you 'knew' that you were the almighty Son of God, with all divine power at your disposal, what would you do? Jesus stoops. In fact, it is *because* all things are 'under his power' that he stoops. He performs the lowliest task imaginable – one reserved for the lowest slave in any household. Jesus notices that no-one has done this menial task of washing feet. No matter, the Son of God will do it. Did you notice that little word 'so' in the passage above? 'Jesus knew … *so* he got up …' That 'so' blows my mind. We're being told that *because* of his almighty stature, *therefore* he stoops. *Because* he is the eternal Son of the Father, *therefore* he serves beneath all human dignity. *Because* he is God, *therefore* he takes the role of a slave.

The man who said, 'Anyone who has seen me has seen the Father' takes off his outer robe, puts on a towel and does the job of the lowest slave. As he comes around the table, you can feel the whole room squirm. Peter voices the mood of everyone:

'Lord, are you going to wash my feet?'
Jesus replied, 'You do not realise now what I am doing, but later you will understand.'
'No,' said Peter, 'you shall never wash my feet' (John 13:6–8).

I get Peter's reaction. I was once in India, staying with a very respectable family in Indian society. The father was a nawab – an Indian prince. While I was there, my hosts were insisting that I had a pedicure. I flatly refused. No way was I going to let someone poke around my carbuncled monstrosities. I didn't want to look down on another human being while they fussed over my dirty feet. It is such an awkward thing to have someone hold your naked feet, to wash water over them and towel them dry while all you can do is sit there and watch. I was uncomfortable at the idea of one of the household servants performing such a task. It would have been unthinkable to imagine my host – this prince – taking off *his* royal robes, wrapping a towel around *his* waist and kneeling at *my* stinking feet. Yet while an earthly prince would not think to stoop like this, on Maundy Thursday the highest King climbed down to the lowest station.

The whole episode is meant to show us 'the full extent of his love'.[10] This is why the scene is full of deeper resonances. Jesus, the Prince of heaven, has been at the place of honour – he has been with his Father and the Holy Spirit from before the beginning of the world.[11] Yet, out of love, he leaves his heavenly place and stoops to our level. On Maundy Thursday Jesus puts himself even lower than his disciples and becomes unclean just to wash them. This is a picture of what was to come the next day. On Good Friday Jesus would descend to the very depths and become spiritually filthy. On the cross Jesus took the very lowest place, dying the most shameful death imaginable. Yet through his death Jesus was taking our sin onto himself so that we might be spiritually cleansed.

The foot washing was a dramatisation of the great love story. Jesus takes the lowest place in order to cleanse us. As we witness this stooping love, we are not seeing a departure from divine glory. As he picks up the towel, Jesus is not taking a holiday from Godhood. This is what true Godhood looks like.

WHAT GOD LOOKS LIKE

To see God we don't gaze up to the heavens; we look down, awkwardly, to the slave at our feet, intent on washing us. There is God, on his knees, getting dirty so we can be clean. There is God, embracing humiliation to dignify us. There is God, at our feet, and none of us know where to look.

You see, none of us deserve this. On the night of the foot washing, every single follower of Jesus will desert, deny or betray him before daybreak. The feet cleansed by Jesus will either run from him or, figuratively, walk all over him. Jesus knows this. Still he stoops. And as he stoops, two things are revealed. We see what *he* is like and we see what *we* are like.

What is Jesus like? He is a million miles from the God who rearranges stars to make us bow. He is the God who gets down on his knees to deal with our mess.

What are we like? In short, we are not like Jesus. We can kid ourselves that we're loving until we see true love in action. I've never washed a grown man's feet and I find it hard to even imagine myself into that position. Yet every day I wash my *own* feet. I care for my own needs without a second thought.

I love people if they are lovely. Jesus loves people because they are not. I love people if it's convenient. Jesus serves others even on the eve of his execution. I care more for my reputation than for those I claim to love. Jesus kneels at our filthy feet no matter the shame, no matter the cost, no matter the protests.

Jesus' love unmasks my love for the sham that it is. And suddenly I realise I need cleansing too. That's why he stoops. And why he suffers ...

4

LOVE SUFFERS

Imagine a homeless man, begging for change. One passer-by bends down to drop a coin into his cup, then hurries on. Another slows to a standstill when he recognises the beggar. 'I can't believe it. Joe? I've found you! Dad will be thrilled.' He sits down in the gutter and puts his arm around his sobbing brother. 'Don't worry, I'll get you home.'

True love stoops. But this stooping is not just a gesture. Stooping is what love does when it sees need. Stooping says, 'Your needs are my needs. Your debts are my debts. Your pain is my pain.' This is why stooping leads to suffering. In fact, love that does not suffer is suspect love. Even our English word 'passion' reflects this. It comes from the Latin *passio*, meaning to suffer. Therefore when love *himself* shows up, he not only stoops but he also suffers. As Jesus approached his own death, he revealed the heights of his love by showing the depths of his suffering.

A SECOND PASSOVER

The night of the foot washing – the night before Jesus died – was the Jewish feast of Passover. It was the most significant date of the Jewish calendar. Passover was the meal where Jews commemorated their deliverance by God from slavery in Egypt. Families would gather around good food, good wine, singing and storytelling. Yet as Jesus went to his death, he added a second level of meaning to the Passover. He used the meal to tell *his* story. As we read in Matthew's Gospel:

> While they were eating, Jesus took bread, and when he had given thanks, he broke it and gave it to his disciples, saying, 'Take and eat; this is my body' (Matthew 26:26).

Just imagine the scene. Jesus takes a loaf in his hands – a loaf which he says 'is my body' – then he tears it apart in front of their eyes. When you understand the symbolism, the violence of this act is shocking. We're seeing the cross dramatised. Jesus, the true Bread of Life, is savagely ripped apart. Why? So he can feed us. He dies so that we can live. He is devoured that we might feast. He is broken that we might be nourished.

Think of a loaf torn apart and handed to you. It is freely offered, life-giving and nourishing. But we only receive this bread because first it is broken. We only enjoy his life because first he dies.

Jesus makes this point again when he takes a cup of wine:

> Then he took a cup, and when he had given thanks, he gave it to them, saying, 'Drink from it, all of you. This is my blood of the covenant, which is poured out for many for the forgiveness of sins (Matthew 26:27–28).

In the Bible wine is twinned with blood. It's called the 'blood of the grape'.[12] At the same time blood is strongly associated with life – so we read elsewhere that 'life … is in the blood'.[13] Indeed, if we see blood pouring out of someone, we know that *life* is pouring out of them. As Jesus pours out the wine he is showing us the life he is about to give on the cross. His body will be torn apart; his blood will be poured out. Jesus will be utterly consumed and exhausted on the cross; he will be broken and expended. Yet Jesus endures death so that we get to feast. He gives his blood so that we enjoy a banquet.

Perhaps you ask, 'Why should Jesus suffer in this way?' The answer is that this is where love takes him. As we have seen, love means saying, 'Your burdens are my burdens.' Jesus enters into suffering and death because this is *our* plight. He goes to the hell of the cross because this is the problem we face – and have done ever since the Garden of Eden. That's why Jesus' next stop on this Thursday night is another garden.

A SECOND GARDEN

After the Passover meal, Jesus goes with his followers to a garden just outside Jerusalem called Gethsemane. It's 'a second garden' because Gethsemane proves to be the answer to the first garden – that is, the Garden of Eden. The Garden of Eden was where the love story went wrong. The Garden of Gethsemane is where it's put right.

Allow me to take you back to 'the scene of the crime'. In that first garden Adam and Eve were king and queen of all creation. They were made by the God of love, made for love and made to rule the world in love. All was paradise. But they spurned that love. They did not trust the God of love, who had provided them with cosmic abundance. God had withheld from them just one tree in all the world – 'the tree of the knowledge of good and evil'[14] – but Adam and Eve fixated on the tiny prohibition and forgot the overflowing provision. They did not trust God and so grasped at life on their own terms. In Genesis chapter 3 we read of them eating the forbidden fruit, and this is what has gone wrong with the world.

Perhaps that sounds out of proportion. Why should eating from the one forbidden tree have such devastating consequences? The Bible answers it like this: the consequences are so drastic because love is so vital – it really does make the world go round. To mess with love messes with everything. This is true on a personal as well as a cosmic level.

On a personal level we see how our own lives go wrong when our loves are twisted. We love the wrong things – those things grip our heart and pervert our loves even further. We love the right things, but we love them out of all proportion or for the wrong reasons. We say we love *that certain someone* but really we love the *idea* of that certain someone, or we love the *feeling* of love, or we love *being seen* to love, or we simply love *ourselves* and the other person is there to boost our ego. Our love so often turns to hate or bitterness. The hatred and bitterness of others compounds our own and so we spiral down.

Love is the greatest thing in life, but there is a flip side to that truth: distorted love is the greatest evil. This is true on a personal level, but the Bible says it has happened at a cosmic level too. God created the world to revolve around love. The relationship between God and humans is the reason for the universe and the axis on which this world turns. When that relationship is good, all is right with the world. When God and humanity are out of sorts, the world is out of kilter – all hell breaks loose. This is what was unleashed in that first garden.

Really we shouldn't be surprised at this. If you turn from the God of love, inevitably this will mean disconnection – from God and from one another. If you turn from the God of light, inevitably this will mean darkness – getting lost in ignorance and sin. If you turn from the God of life, inevitably this will mean death – not just the ceasing of our heartbeats but a spiritual death too: a separation from God. Ever since the first garden, this has been the life that we've known – a life of disconnection, darkness and death.

Trace back the avalanche of evil in this world to its source and you'll find a single snowflake tipping the balance. One man, Adam, mistrusted God. In that original garden there was a 'declaration of independence'. In rebellion Adam went to a tree to serve himself, and a world of pain has been the result. Ever since then we have struggled in Adam's suffering world and shared in Adam's selfish ways.

Step forward the hero of the story. Step forward a second Adam who enters a second garden. When Jesus goes into the garden of Gethsemane on this Thursday night, he is a champion entering the fray. Everyone else has gone the way of Adam – all of us have been selfish, and as a result we've all suffered and we're all headed for death. But Jesus has come to reverse the way of Adam. Where Adam selfishly grasped at his tree and brought disaster on the world, Jesus has come to selflessly embrace his tree – the cross – and bring salvation to the world.

As Jesus enters this second garden, the stakes could not be higher. He is intensely aware of the fight ahead of him and the suffering it will entail. He describes it as his 'cup'.

A SECOND CUP

We pick up the story in Matthew chapter 26:

> Then Jesus went with his disciples to a place called Gethsemane, and he said to them, 'Sit here while I go over there and pray.' He took Peter and the two sons of Zebedee along with him, and he began to be sorrowful and troubled. Then he said to them, 'My soul is overwhelmed with sorrow to the point of death. Stay here and keep watch with me.'
>
> Going a little farther, he fell with his face to the ground and prayed, 'My Father, if it is possible, may this cup be taken from me. Yet not as I will, but as you will' (Matthew 26:36–39).

What is this 'cup' that Jesus prays about? It's not a literal cup. It's a way of describing the suffering of the cross which Jesus is about to undergo. He knows that he is about to endure the consequences of our disconnection, darkness and death. He's about to go to the place where all our sin takes us – he's about to suffer hell for us. That's the meaning of this poisoned chalice and it's why Jesus is so overwhelmed.

The Bible speaks of this cup a number of times. Here is one description:

> In the hand of the Lord is a cup
> full of foaming wine mixed with spices;
> he pours it out, and all the wicked of the earth
> drink it down to its very dregs
> (Psalm 75:8).

Imagine the whole world queuing up for this cup. Humanity has walked away from the God of love, light and life, and now it must drink down the consequences – disconnection, darkness and death. Imagine the contents of this cup – all hell is distilled in it. Now imagine your place in the queue. You are moving step by step closer to it. Ahead you look beyond the cup to see Jesus. He's not in the queue; it's not his cup to drink. But there he is kneeling down in front of it in profound anguish. He is facing the prospect of drinking it *for us.*

Luke's Gospel records that Jesus was sweating blood as he prepared to drink from it.[15] Doctors today call this condition Hematidrosis and it occurs rarely in situations of extreme emotional pressure. Essentially blood vessels are bursting all over his body and mingling with the sweat as it pours scarlet from his face. He does not want to drink this cup. What a different cup this is from the cup of wine which, earlier in the night, Jesus had offered to his disciples. That cup was full of forgiveness; this cup is full of judgement. That cup signals life; this cup brings death. That cup Jesus offers to us; this cup he drinks himself.

This is why Jesus prays:

> My Father, if it is not possible for this cup to be taken away unless I drink it, may your will be done (Matthew 26:42).

To understand the prospect before Jesus just put your finger over the first three words of that verse. The truth is that it is not possible for the cup to be taken away *unless Jesus drinks it*. Either he drains this cup to its dregs or else we must drink it. Either he takes our judgement or we must. Either he suffers for our sins or we suffer.

In this garden love stooped. Love came all the way down into our suffering plight. Love prayed for us. Love agonised over us. And love resolved to do *anything* to save us: to pay any cost and to bear any pain. As Jesus contemplates dying on the cross, the situation is this: either he drinks the cup or we do; either he faces divine judgement or we do; either he suffers hell or we do. And in this garden Jesus resolves, 'Father, let it be me.'

This is love. Love stoops and love suffers. Why? Because love sacrifices.

5

LOVE SACRIFICES

'God is love' says a famous Bible verse.[16] I wonder how you react to that? It's a saying that tends to split opinion. Some scoff at the idea. In a world of pain, who can really believe in a loving God? It may seem like a cruel joke to speak of a God of pure love when the world is far from pure and anything but lovely.

On the other hand, there are people who adopt the phrase as their personal motto. 'God is love' is the sort of sentiment that gets cross-stitched on to Grandma's wall hangings. It's found on the lips of the spiritual guru and in the Facebook updates of your church-going auntie. So when you hear the phrase 'God is love', how do you respond? Do you loathe it or love it? Is the idea cruel or cool? Is it bunk or brilliant?

The first thing to say about this divide is that both sides are in danger of misunderstanding the phrase. Both views are liable to see love as a feeling. One side sees it as a sentiment too flimsy for the real world of struggle and death. The other side can see love as an emotional novocaine – a lovely, numbing sensation that gets you through this world of pain. But we all know that love worthy of the name is a deeper reality. Real love does not ignore the darkness but meets us in it.

The love which the Bible speaks about is earthed in blood, sweat and tears. The verse that says 'God is love' goes on immediately to say:

This is how God showed his love among us: he sent his one and only Son into the world that we might live through him (1 John 4:9).

Love does not remain at a distance and merely gush with oaths of undying affection; love stoops. It does not remain aloof or abstract; love comes down. Love shares our kind of life so that we can share his kind of life. That's what this verse is saying and it's what we've been exploring in the last two chapters. Jesus came into the world to bring us the love of heaven. Ultimately, though, it's not Jesus' *life* that reveals the depths of God's love; it's his death. The love that stooped to suffer is a love that came to sacrifice. It's a love that was always headed to Good Friday – always headed towards the cross. This is what the next verse goes on to say:

> This is love: not that we loved God, but that he loved us and sent his Son as an atoning sacrifice for our sins (1 John 4:10).

If I asked you to picture love, perhaps you'd imagine a kiss, or a mother with her child, or an elderly couple hand in hand. In the Bible, if you want to picture love, you should bring to mind the cross. Below we will read Matthew's account of the crucifixion. From one perspective it is a record of shocking brutality, but when viewed from God's perspective it is something more – it is heroic. It is the ultimate sacrifice. It is an act of pure love:

They stripped him and put a scarlet robe on him, and then twisted together a crown of thorns and set it on his head. They put a staff in his right hand. Then they knelt in front of him and mocked him. 'Hail, king of the Jews!' they said. They spat on him, and took the staff and struck him on the head again and again. After they had mocked him, they took off the robe and put his own clothes on him. Then they led him away to crucify him ...

Two rebels were crucified with him, one on his right and one on his left. Those who passed by hurled insults at him, shaking their heads and saying, 'You who are going to destroy the temple and build it in three days, save yourself! Come down from the cross, if you are the Son of God!' In the same way the chief priests, the teachers of the law and the elders mocked him. 'He saved others,' they said, 'but he can't save himself! He's the king of Israel! Let him come down now from the cross, and we will believe in him. He trusts in God. Let God rescue him now if he wants him, for he said, "I am the Son of God."' In the same way the rebels who were crucified with him also heaped insults on him.

From noon until three in the afternoon darkness came over all the land. About three in the afternoon Jesus cried out in a loud voice, *'Eli, Eli, lema sabachthani?'* (which means 'My God, my God, why have you forsaken me?') (Matthew 27:28–31, 38–46).

What on earth does this have to do with love? Mockery, torture, shame, pain and death seem about as far from popular conceptions of love as it's possible to be. How can our earlier Bible passage say, 'This is how God showed his love among us'? It can say this because of how the next verse ends. The cross is 'an atoning sacrifice for our sins'.

Jesus' death might look futile or fearful from one perspective, but from another it looks like heart-melting devotion. Think of the soldier who throws himself on a grenade. Without context you might see this as a desperate waste, a tragic accident or an act of suicide, but look at the bigger picture and you'll see that he's sacrificing himself to save his friends. This is just the way Jesus describes his own death:

> Greater love has no one than this: to lay down one's life for one's friends. You are my friends (John 15:13–14).

People may view the cross as a desperate waste, a tragic accident or even an act of suicide, but Jesus wants us to look again at it. This is actually the supreme expression of befriending love. He's throwing himself on the grenade, so to speak. On the cross Jesus sacrifices himself for us.

We keep using the word 'sacrifice'. What does it mean? That's what we will next examine.

THE SACRIFICES OF OLD

Picture the scene. You're an Israelite living during the Old Testament times. Let's say you're living eight centuries before the first Christmas. You have come to the holiest place in the world – the temple – and, in recognition of your guilt before God, you have brought with you a sacrifice. As you draw near to the God of life, light and love, your own death, darkness and disconnection becomes ever more apparent. The light of God reveals the darkness of your heart. This is always the way. Any time you enter the presence of greatness you feel inadequate, so how much more is this true when you enter the presence of God?

Therefore, as you draw near to a God who blazes with goodness, you begin to feel how different you are – how *bad* you are. You realise you should 'get it in the neck' for the disaster you've made of your life and relationships. But this is why you've brought your sacrifice. Now, instead of *you* getting it in the neck, Flossy the sheep takes the hit.

Perhaps you're thinking, 'Poor Flossy! What did Flossy ever do to deserve that?' That's the point. Flossy is innocent. You are guilty. But the sacrifice dies in your place. You therefore experience undeserved mercy, while the sheep experiences undeserved judgement. Before you object about this treatment of animals, let's be honest: Flossy was always going to die. Today we still kill our sheep, it's just that in Old Testament times the butcher (a.k.a. 'priest') added a level of theatre to proceedings. Before they turned their livestock into dinner the Old Testament believers went through a ritual that pointed them to Christ's sacrifice. They knew that animals couldn't atone for our guilt, but for hundreds of years beforehand they acted out the drama of the cross. When Jesus – the promised Saviour – finally arrived in the flesh, John the Baptist was able to announce: 'Look, the Lamb of God, who takes away the sin of the world!'[17] That's who Jesus is: the ultimate Flossy. He gets it in the neck so that we go free.

Every Old Testament sacrifice was preparing the people for Jesus. Their lambs, goats and bulls could not really pay for sin, but those sacrifices were proclaiming Easter. And today, as we reflect on those old sacrifices, we can still learn much about the cross.

THE CROSS ACCORDING TO THE TEMPLE

Let's go back to the scene we imagined earlier. You are in the temple – in 800 BC– and you're queuing up to confess your sins to a priest. You have your lamb at the ready. When the time is right, you will lay it on the altar and put your hands on its head, confessing your sins over the animal. This is the idea of putting your guilt on to the sacrifice. *Then* you will put a knife to its neck.

Yet before you get to all that, you hear a booming voice from the heart of the temple. It's the Lord – the Almighty Son of God – and he says to everyone in the temple courts, 'Get out!' You pick up a relieved Flossy and run to a safe distance. You turn back and see the Lord Jesus step down from his throne room, descend through the holy places and come out into the courtyard, the place of sacrifice. Astonishingly, *he* lays down on the altar. He calls over a trembling priest and gets him to lay hands on his head. The priest obliges, confessing the sins of all the people and laying them on Jesus. Then, carrying the guilt of all the people, Jesus is slain, and the blood that pours down that altar is the crimson flow of God's love.

This is what happens in the 'passion' of Jesus Christ. This is what love looks like – it looks like the cross, where Jesus was sacrificed once and for all as the Lamb of God. He takes what we deserve, so that we get what he deserves. He endures our judgement, so that we get his mercy. He dies, so that we may live.

You actually could not tell a greater love story than this. No other romance has such an exalted hero who plunges to such depths. Here is the Lord, our Maker, suffering our hell so that we might have heaven. As the Bible declares: 'Greater love has no one than this ...'[18] for 'This is love: not that we loved God, but that he loved us and sent his Son as an atoning sacrifice for our sins.'[19]

ALL LOVE IS SACRIFICIAL

I hope you are seeing something of the wonder of Christ's sacrifice, but perhaps you're experiencing a problem in this chapter. You can agree that love stoops. You can even see how love suffers. Yet perhaps you have an issue with sacrifice. Does it seem to you like a brutal and Bronze-Age concept? All this talk of blood and the bearing of judgement – isn't that at odds with love? As we finish this chapter, let me say a resounding 'No'. In fact, let me insist that all love that's worthy of the name is sacrificial.

If the soldier is going to love his friends, it will mean the ultimate sacrifice – throwing himself on the grenade. Out of love, he will suffer so that others may live. Or if the lender is going to love the one who cannot pay them back, it will mean sacrifice – out of love, the lender will forgive the debt. She 'takes the hit' financially; her love says, 'Let it be me.' Likewise, if I'm going to love you when you've wronged me, this will mean sacrifice – I will forgive you. That will be costly – it will mean not making you pay. I will have to refrain from gossiping about you. I will have to wish you well when I want to bear a grudge. To love means to sacrifice: that's just how it works.

Allow me to illustrate with a final analogy. Plenty of love stories tell the tale of the

Prince and the Pauper. We can see the cross as the ultimate telling of this story. Imagine the Prince falling in love with an unfortunate commoner. He pledges himself to her in marriage. What happens when they marry? They share everything. The marriage vows say, 'All that I am I give to you; and all that I have I share with you.' So as the Pauper says this, all her debts are going to the Prince. He absorbs them all, paying them off in full. At the same time the Prince vows his all to the Pauper and in that moment his riches are hers. The Prince happily pays the price to be with his beloved. This is a sacrifice he gladly bears, and through this loving union he takes all that is hers and gives her all that is his.

This is what is happening on the cross. Think of the one hanging there, covered in blood and spittle. He is the Prince of heaven with his arms wide open to the world. He has stooped, he has suffered and he has sacrificed, all to be with you. As you look to Jesus, can you doubt that he loves you? Can you doubt that he is given to you? Can you doubt that he has taken your debts – your sins – and given you himself in return? There, in Jesus, is the love of God for you.

How do you react to this love? As you hear his vows, declared from the cross, will you respond in kind? I hope you might respond with a prayer like this:

Lord Jesus, you have won me. You have given yourself to me with every drop of your blood. I love you. I tell you now that I belong to you, body and soul. All that that I am I give to you, and all that I have I share with you – for better, for worse, for richer, for poorer, in sickness and in health, till death *and beyond*. Amen.

This kind of prayer is simply the most appropriate response to a love that has gone to hell and back for you. Whether you have been a Christian for many years or whether you're only now understanding God's love, this is what faith looks like. Faith is the response which God's love wins from our hearts. Perhaps it's happening in you even as you read this now.

You may have found yourself saying 'Amen' to the prayer above. If so, you are finding yourself in the ultimate love story. You have caught sight of the great hero and you're beginning to see yourself as the beloved. This is the meaning of life: 'to know this love that surpasses knowledge'.[20]

And there's more. This love is not just yours now; this love stands forever. There really is a 'happily ever after'.

6

LOVE STANDS

Doomed love is a familiar story. Think of William Shakespeare's *Romeo and Juliet*. Those 'star-crossed lovers' attempted to bridge the chasm of two warring families. Would their love be enough? No, it didn't end well. Not every love story is a comedy. Many are tragic. In *Romeo and Juliet* it's not love that wins but death.

How does our story end? Is it any different? So far we have seen love stoop, suffer and sacrifice. But will it all end in tragedy? Was the cross ultimately a doomed gesture by Jesus – displaying his love in a dying cause?

The Old Testament contains an extended love poem called 'The Song of Songs'. In it a question emerges about which is stronger: love or death?[21] I wonder what you think. The romantic in us wants to believe that love is stronger. The realist – especially if we've just lost a loved one – laments that death wins in the end. So what's the truth?

As that first Easter Sunday dawned, it looked to everyone like death was the winner. Jesus' followers were not waiting outside the tomb, champagne glasses primed, ready to toast an almighty victory over the grave. No, these men and women had seen his bloodied corpse taken down from the cross and laid in a cold, dark tomb. To them it seemed like love had stooped, suffered and sacrificed but that now love was dead. And they expected to be next.

On Easter Sunday they were cowering away from the authorities that had just killed their leader. In spite of all Jesus' teaching on the subject (and he was very clear that he would rise from the dead), the last thing they expected was to see him again. But then John's Gospel reports the following:

On the evening of that first day of the week, when the disciples were together, with the doors locked for fear of the Jewish leaders, Jesus came and stood among them and said, 'Peace be with you!' After he said this, he showed them his hands and side. The disciples were overjoyed when they saw the Lord. Again Jesus said, 'Peace be with you!' (John 20:19–21).

Put yourself in the sandals of these followers of Jesus. None of them had covered themselves in glory when Jesus was arrested and tried. In fact they had all deserted and denied him in his hour of need. Yet now he's back from beyond the grave! Having survived death, he tracks down these worthless traitors. What will he say to them? 'Peace!' he says. This is his number-one post-resurrection greeting. Love stoops, suffers and sacrifices, then love stands again on the far side of death preaching peace even to gutless deserters.

If some random corpse returned to life, that would be earth-shattering enough. But the Easter story is not simply that 'an individual' beat death. Easter tells us that *Jesus* rose, that *Peace* came back from the dead, that *Love* has conquered the grave.

This can be hard to believe, though. And 'Doubting Thomas' – one of the twelve disciples – speaks up for all sceptics. He was not there to see the original Easter appearance, and so he airs his doubts:

> Now Thomas (also known as Didymus), one of the Twelve, was not with the disciples when Jesus came. So the other disciples told him, 'We have seen the Lord!'

> But he said to them, 'Unless I see the nail marks in his hands and put my finger where the nails were, and put my hand into his side, I will not believe' (John 20:24–25).

You can understand Thomas's reaction. Dead men don't rise! Death is stronger than love, right? But Jesus appears to Thomas to upend all his assumptions:

A week later his disciples were in the house again, and Thomas was with them. Though the doors were locked, Jesus came and stood among them and said, 'Peace be with you!' Then he said to Thomas, 'Put your finger here; see my hands. Reach out your hand and put it into my side. Stop doubting and believe.'

Thomas said to him, 'My Lord and my God!' (John 20:26–28)

This is how Thomas came to believe in the resurrection. It was not by mathematical proofs, not via scientific experiments and not even through a miraculous demonstration of heavenly power. The proof that turned 'Doubting Thomas' into a believer was the *scars* of Jesus. These wounds tell a scar story – a story about Jesus stooping, suffering, sacrificing and then standing again on the far side of death. Thomas is not simply persuaded about an afterlife. Thomas meets his battle-scarred friend and is assured that Jesus has fought to the death for him. It's an all-conquering love that overwhelms Thomas and he cries out, 'My Lord and my God!'

LIFE FROM THE DEAD

Jesus' appearance to Thomas was part of a six-week resurrection roadshow. For forty days after Easter Sunday, Jesus spoke with hundreds, ate meals, shared long walks, went fishing with friends and held barbecues on the beach.[22] In all he did he was offering a foretaste of the future. The life beyond death which Jesus pioneers is not about spiritual vibes in the seventh dimension; it's about friendship and feasting. It is earthy, physical and filled with joy.

Perhaps you're thinking, 'Sounds great! I'm just not sure I can believe in it.' In this next section, let me suggest to you that you already believe in resurrection. Whatever your religious convictions – or lack thereof – you hold to some kind of Easter story. To account for the world around you, for the history that's shaped you and the heart that drives you, you already believe in 'life from the dead'. Actually it's the Christian story of 'life from the dead' that makes sense of how you live – it's the *true* love story that makes sense of the others. I'll show you what I mean as I highlight three areas: the heavens, history and our hearts.

1. THE HEAVENS

This universe is a life-from-the-dead kind of universe – it is an Easter type of a cosmos. If you don't believe in the Easter God, you end up having to believe in some really extraordinary life-from-the-dead miracles to account for it:

Miracle 1: the universe came into existence from nothing and for no reason.

Miracle 2: the harmony of the cosmos emerged from chaos, and without a cause.

Miracle 3: life materialised from non-life purely via mechanical / chemical processes.

Miracle 4: our minds have developed from mindless matter.

All of these are about life from the dead. But if there is not a life-from-the-dead *God* behind these phenomena, they turn out to be the most incredible miracles ever proposed by humanity. Without a life-from-the-dead God, these occurrences are really flat-out absurdities.

Compare this with the Easter miracle: the resurrection. That too is about life from the dead. But the Easter miracle has a miracle-*maker* – the God of love. It also has a *meaning* – it is part of the great love story. Within this love story the Easter miracle makes sense. In fact it begins to make sense of those other miracles too. It assures us that we live in a life-from-the-dead cosmos because there is a life-from-the-dead God – Jesus' resurrection is proof of it. In this way we see that his resurrection is not absurd or irrational, rather it explains what would *otherwise* be absurd and irrational.

2. HISTORY

The history told by the Scriptures is clear and even the great majority of historians can agree to its basic facts. These facts are as follows. Jesus was (at the very least) a prophet who gained a following in Judea and Galilee. He was at the centre of controversy in Jerusalem around AD 30. He was tried and put to death under the Roman governor Pontius Pilate. Having been executed, he was placed in a tomb, the whereabouts of which was common knowledge. On the third day after his death the tomb was empty and his followers began to have experiences of the risen Christ. Those experiences went on for forty days and then stopped when they claimed he had returned to heaven. The body was never found and the Christian movement began right away in Jerusalem – the preaching of the empty tomb being a key foundation. These preachers of Christ's resurrection were powerless and unschooled, nonetheless they maintained their testimony under great persecution – some even to the point of death. Against all odds the Christian movement mushroomed in size. It has become the largest, most diverse society in history and its central proclamation has always been this Easter story.

These are the simple facts of history. Conspiracy theorists may propose alternative explanations – such as that Jesus passed out on the cross and revived in the cool of the tomb, or that the disciples stole the body and lied about it, or that they were all hallucinating – but none of those explanations properly fit the facts. It turns out that the Easter story is by far the most convincing explanation for the facts of history.

What's more, the history of the church *since* Easter Sunday is a powerful argument for the truth of its message. When you consider that Jesus died in ignominy in his early thirties – leaving no army, no political party, no published works and no schools – it's difficult to understand how the Jesus movement survived his death. He had no shred of earthly power, wealth or influence. He was a nobody followed by no-hopers, and yet he is the central figure of human history. How could this happen? The Jesus movement has exploded on to the world stage and continues to mushroom in size. It's worth trying to trace back this 'blast' to its origin. When was 'ground zero' from which all this activity began? Undoubtedly it was Easter Sunday. Before then the Jesus movement had no global impact. Afterwards – straight afterwards – we can trace the extraordinary growth of history's greatest sociological movement. What caused this? It certainly wasn't the genius or political wiles of the disciples. They were unschooled fishermen, notorious sinners, enemies of the state and despised commoners. Somehow, though, they managed to pen the most earth-shattering, civilisation-shaping work in all literature – the New Testament – and to genuinely turn the world upside down. Before Easter Sunday they were deserting and denying Jesus, cowering away in the shadows. After Easter they conquer the world. Something happened that Sunday to change them. What was it? The most straightforward and credible explanation is the one they insist on: Jesus really did rise from the dead.

3. OUR HEARTS

We have considered the heavens above and history around us. We now turn to our hearts within. Here we find a powerful testimony to resurrection – an unavoidable sense that love is indeed stronger than death.

We all live as though love is ultimate. Everyone knows we should prioritise relationships: when they are good, life is very good; when they are bad, it is awful. Love rules in our *hearts*, but is that just wishful thinking?

With the resurrection we have grounds for taking our dearest intuitions seriously. If Jesus rose again, then this life-from-the-dead God really does reign and his love story really will prevail. That gives us warrant for our heartfelt convictions. Yet without Easter faith we ought to conclude that life is a brief moment in the sun which the darkness will then swallow. Such a philosophy is, in the end, unliveable.

Very few people are nihilists, who believe that life is meaningless, and even fewer live consistently with that nihilism. Most of us carry on as though life is greater than death, as though love trumps disconnection, as though light triumphs over darkness. This is why we tell all the stories that we do. Whatever we believe, we cannot cope without stories of love, life and light triumphing – our hearts demand it. We live as though Easter is true!

Since this is the case, we are faced with a choice, but not between the 'myth' of Easter and the 'reality' of a secular worldview. Our choice is really between the one 'myth' that claims to have shown up in history – that of Jesus – and all the other myths we tell ourselves to get us through the night. When viewed like this we realise that belief in the resurrection is not the absurdity; it's what explains what would otherwise be absurd. Our hearts make sense when Easter is embraced.

So, then, our universe is a life-from-the-dead universe, our history is a life-from-the-dead history and our heartfelt convictions are life-from-the-dead convictions. Is it really so difficult to believe in a life-from-the-dead God? What would stop you from looking to Jesus and declaring what Thomas declared: 'My Lord and my God'?

Perhaps you are thinking, 'It was alright for Thomas. He got to *see* Jesus. What about me?' Actually Jesus addresses that issue directly.

ENTERING THE STORY

John's account of the Thomas story continues:

> Then Jesus told Thomas, 'Because you have seen me, you have believed; blessed are those who have not seen and yet have believed' (John 20:29).

You might think that Thomas was incredibly 'blessed' to get the proof he asked for, but Jesus doesn't call Thomas 'blessed'. According to Jesus, the blessed people are those who *don't* see him and yet believe. You and I were not there when the risen Jesus showed up, but Jesus says, essentially, 'That's alright, it's better that way.' How is it better? John provides the answer:

> ... *these [things] are written* that you may believe that Jesus is the Messiah, the Son of God, and that by believing you may have life in his name (John 20:31, emphasis added).

The Bible (of which John's Gospel is a part) has been given so that we can have an experience like Thomas. These things are written so that we might believe. And this is the 'blessed' way to encounter Jesus. It's better.

'Better?' you ask. How could reading of Jesus in the Bible be better than seeing him in the flesh? Well, just imagine that Jesus appeared to you tonight at the end of your bed. Imagine you saw his wounds and heard him say 'Peace' to you personally. That would give you a spiritual high for days. Weeks, even! But quite soon you'd start to wonder whether you'd dreamt the whole thing. People would ridicule you for your claims. Fairly shortly you'd need another appearance. If you have ever asked for an extraordinary appearance of God, you are asking for something that will impress you today but will ultimately make you doubt more than believe.

It is more blessed – it is better – to go on the eye-witness testimony of the Bible. With the Bible's accounts Jesus' words are there in black and white for all time: when you have doubts; when it's three in the morning; when a loved one dies; or when you've lost your job. You can always 'see Jesus' by opening the Bible and encountering him in that ancient love story.

This is how J.R.R. Tolkien met with Jesus, and it's how C.S. Lewis met him. It's how I met with Jesus, and how millions of others across the world and down through the ages have done so. We have opened the Bible, seen the hero of heroes and been swept up in the story. I wonder if the same has happened to you?

As we have thought about the Bible's story, perhaps you have seen something of Jesus. Have you sensed his authority? Does it seem to you like this Jesus really is the hero of heroes? Does it make sense to you that Jesus, and his love story, is greater than death, or do you think that death is greater than Jesus? Are you starting to call him, 'My Lord and my God'?

If not, let me point you back to the eye-witness testimony – the Gospels. Perhaps start with John's Gospel as, after all, it was written 'that you may believe'. Read this love story, written by somebody who saw first-hand all that Jesus did. Maybe you could even shoot up a prayer to God as you read: 'Dear God, show me the truth. Show me your love. Show me your

Son.' It's a no-lose prayer. If God isn't there, he won't hear you. But if he is, then there's nothing more important than meeting him.

If you have been moved by these things, God's love story is doing its work. If you are starting to see the love of Jesus, I would urge you to respond. Call out to the God of Easter now. Perhaps you could use words like this:

Dear God, you are light; I have darkness. You are life; I'm surrounded by death. You are love; I am disconnected. I'm sorry for the way I have sinned against you. With your help I want to turn from that darkness, death and disconnection and turn to Jesus. Thank you that Jesus, your Son, has stooped, suffered, sacrificed and stood again on the far side of death. Thank you that he has loved me with every drop of his blood, paying the price for my sins. I believe Jesus is 'my Lord and my God'. I recognise him as the Prince of heaven who has won me back. Please receive me as your child, fill me with your Spirit and be my loving Father forever. Amen.

If you have prayed a prayer like this or you would like to know more about the great love story of Easter, please get in contact: glen@speaklife.org.uk.

NOTES

I. TRUE STORY

[1] Humphrey Carpenter, *The Inklings: C.S. Lewis, J.R.R. Tolkien, Charles Williams, and Their Friends* (Boston: Houghton Mifflin, 1979), pp. 42–43.

[2] Letter from 18 October 1931.

[3] C.S. Lewis, *God in the Dock* (Grand Rapids, Michigan: William B. Eerdmans Publishing Company, 1970), p. 66.

[4] For references to Pontius Pilate in the Bible see Luke 3:1 and Acts 4:27.

[5] C.S. Lewis, *God in the Dock*, p. 158.

2. BACK STORY

6   Genesis 1:28, as translated in the King James Bible.

7   Genesis 2:23.

8   William Shakespeare, A Midsummer Night's Dream.

3. LOVE STOOPS

9   Psalm 19:1.

10   John 13:1, as translated in the 1984 version of the NIV.

11   Jesus' existence before the beginning of the world is mentioned in places like John 1:1: 'In the beginning was the Word [Jesus], and the Word was with God, and the Word was God.' Jesus personally makes the claim in places like John 17:24 when he prays to God the Father: '[Y]ou loved me before the creation of the world.' It is the consistent teaching of the Bible that Jesus is older than the universe. Even before the world began he was present with God the Father and the Holy Spirit.

4. LOVE SUFFERS

[12] Deuteronomy 32:14.

[13] Leviticus 17:11.

[14] Genesis 2:16–17.

[15] See Luke 22:44.

5. LOVE SACRIFICES

[16] 1 John 4:8.

[17] John 1:29.

[18] John 15:13.

[19] 1 John 4:10.

[20] Ephesians 3:19.

6. LOVE STANDS

[21] Song of Songs 8:6.

[22] See, for example, the accounts given by Luke (in chapter 24 of his Gospel) and John (chapters 20 and 21).

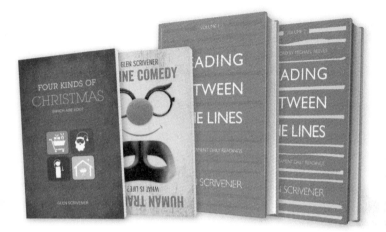